Published by Quickfind Books, a division of Quickread Distribution LLC, Tucson AZ, USA. First edition published as an ebook in March, 2013 by Quickfind Books, Tucson, AZ and Vancouver, BC. First print edition published simultaneously by Quickfind Books through createspace, an Amazon company.

The text of this book is © Wendy Craig, Debra Pepler, Joanne Cummings.

The illustrations are used with permission.

Cover design by Atuzee Media Productions Ltd. Cover illustration used with permission.

Edited by AustinRand, editor and publisher of Quickfind Books.

ISBN: 978-1482562774

From each purchase of this book a royalty is paid to

Authors and contributors

The following authors have been the creators of this book, together with the contributors listed below.

Dr. Wendy Craig is a Professor in the Department of Psychology at Queen's University in Kingston, Ontario, Canada, and is Scientific Co-Director of PREVNet (Promoting Relationships and Eliminating Violence Network). PREVNet is a knowledge-mobilization network focused on reducing violence. Dr. Craig received her Ph.D. in Clinical Developmental Psychology from York University in Toronto, in 1993.

Dr. Craig's research program focuses on: healthy relationships among children, adolescents and adults; bullying and victimization; evaluating violence prevention programs; and knowledge mobilization.

She has received a number of awards in recognition of her work, including an Investigator Award from the Canadian Institute of Health Research; the Canadian Psychological Association Award for Distinguished Contributions to Community Service; the York University Award Redefining the Possible; the Queen's University Excellence in Research Prize, and the Queen Elizabeth Diamond Jubilee Medal.

Dr. Craig has published over 80 scientific articles, 33 book chapters and four edited books. She regularly speaks to parents, educators and professionals working with youth. She has given invited talks in Canada and internationally. As a Canadian representative, Dr. Craig works with the World Health Organization (WHO) conducting research on promoting healthy relationships.

Dr. Debra Pepler is a Distinguished Professor of Psychology at York University and a Senior Executive Member of the LaMarsh Centre for Child and Youth Research, both in Toronto. She is also a Scientific Co-Director of PREVNet. At the Hospital for Sick Children, in Toronto, Dr. Pepler is a Senior Adjunct Scientist. She received her Ph.D. from the University of Waterloo (Ontario) in 1979.

Dr. Pepler conducts research on children at risk. Her major research program examines antisocial behavior of children and adolescents, particularly in school contexts and with their peers. A key aspect of this research was observing interactions among school-aged children with remote microphones and video cameras. Her current research in this area examines aggression and victimization among children and adolescents, with a focus on the processes involved in these problems over the lifespan.

Dr. Pepler consults to SNAP Girls Connection -- a program for aggressive girls and their parents at the Child Development Institute, to Breaking the Cycle – a program for substance-using mothers and their young children, and to Pine River Institute – a program for substance addicted youth. Dr. Pepler has served on several advisory committees focused on parenting, antisocial behavior, and safe school policies, within Canada and internationally.

Dr. Joanne Cummings is the Clinical Director of Psychology at Blueballoon Health Services in Toronto, and the Director of Knowledge Mobilization at PREVNet. She received her Ph.D. in Clinical Developmental Psychology from York University in 2001 and is a member of the College of Psychology of Ontario. Her research has focused on family violence, parenting, and the evaluation of different kinds of therapeutic interventions for parents. Dr. Cummings has been involved in Bullying Prevention Activities since 1995, and has worked with numerous organizations to raise awareness and foster positive social climates and healthy relationships for children and youth. A sought-after public speaker, Joanne has given over 100 presentations and workshops throughout Ontario . Before joining PREVNet, Dr. Cummings was an Ontario Mental Health Postdoctoral Fellow and a Researcher in the Department of Psychiatry at the Hospital for Sick Children, in Toronto, where she evaluated a parent-child psychotherapy intervention and an attachment-focused parenting group for new parents.

In addition to her work with PREVNet, Dr. Cummings has a busy clinical practice working with children and their parents. Dr. Cummings has lectured in the Infant Mental Health Certificate Program at York University and has consulted to the Healthy Babies Healthy Children Program of Toronto Public Health.

The following students of social relationships and bullying prevention have also contributed to this book. Each contributor's academic affiliation is given in brackets.

Lindsey Barrieau (Concordia University), Christine Blain-Arcaro (University of Ottawa), Heather Brittain (McMaster University), Tracy Desjardins (University of Victoria), Dilys Haner (York University), Jennifer Hepditch (University of Ottawa), Lisa Ihnat (University of Ottawa), Amanda Krygsman (McMaster University), Heather McCuaig Edge (Queen's University), Christine Polihronis (Brock University), Michelle Searle (Queen's University), Jessica Trach (University of British Columbia), Gillian Watson (Simon Fraser University).

In addition, the authors thank Patricia Sculthorpe for her contributions to this book.

Bullying prevention: what parents need to know

By Susan Swearer, Ph.D.

"One of the deep secrets of life is that all that is really worth the doing is what we do for others."
-Lewis Carroll

This PREVNet Pocket Guide to Bullying Prevention is a gift for anyone wanting an authoritative, comprehensive, and easily accessible guide to dealing with bullying. Written by three of the top bullying prevention and intervention experts in North America, Drs. Wendy Craig, Debra Pepler and Joanne Cummings, this guide devises realistic strategies for understanding bullying, responding effectively to bullying, and ultimately, ending bullying.

Bullying is not a new phenomenon; yet the international attention to this issue has reached an unprecedented crescendo in the recent decades. Media attention to this phenomenon has exponentially increased since several school shootings in the United States in the 1990s. The 1997 murder of Canadian schoolgirl, Reena Virk, raised national attention to the disastrous consequences of bullying and to the complexity and interaction between social, verbal, and physical bullying. In 2011, the Obama administration convened the first-ever White House conference on bullying prevention, bringing together parents, teachers, youth, politicians, researchers, foundation leaders, and industry leaders to collectively discuss effective strategies for bullying prevention. Yet despite the massive increase in research in bullying and legislative efforts to provide effective policies to respond to bullying, the problem still exists in many schools, families, and communities.

The PREVNet Pocket Guide is the first book in North America to provide easily accessible, research-based information on bullying for parents. The book also is the first to describe bullying from preschool through late adolescence, which provides parents with a "must-have" resource that they can use throughout their children's developmental stages. The book also provides much-needed guidance for parents and students who are struggling with electronic bullying, which has increased in the past decade due to availability of computers, smart phones, and social networking. Parents struggle with maintaining a balance between allowing their adolescents autonomy while navigating the realities of the electronic, networked world in which young people live. Unfortunately, the proliferation of networked gaming, social networking, and smart phones has opened up new avenues for bullying and one which befuddles many adults, who might not be as aware of this networked world. The PREVNet Pocket Guide provides sage guidance for adults dealing with all forms of bullying and recognizes that many forms of bullying occur simultaneously.

Researchers and practitioners have moved beyond the conversation that bullying is detrimental and that bullying exists across the lifespan. We know that as humans negotiate their social relationships, bullying can result if the relationships are negative. Bullying can occur from preschool through adulthood; bullying can occur between youth; bullying can occur in families; bullying can occur between adults and youth. The PREVNet Pocket Guide walks the reader through this reality: bullying is a social relationship problem.

The PREVNet Pocket Guide distills the research on bullying and frames bullying as a relationship problem. The authors wisely advise everyone to practice the golden rule of treating others as they wish to be treated. This simple, yet very profound framing of bullying presents all of us with an important deep secret in life: when relationships are healthy and positive, bullying will not exist.

Susan M. Swearer, Ph.D.
Professor of School Psychology
Co-Director, Bullying Research Network
University of Nebraska - Lincoln

CHAPTER 1
About bullying — basics

Bullying is a relationship problem; the solutions come from making changes in relationships.

What is bullying?

Bullying is aggression carried out repeatedly by an individual (or group) who has more power than the individual who is being victimized and wants to demonstrate this power to the victimized person or to other people. The power arises from within the relationship between the person bullying and the person being bullied. But it also comes from peer bystanders, who are almost always present during bullying episodes.

Bullying is a relationship that is characterized by disrespect. It is a problem relationship because:

- Children who bully are learning to use power and aggression to control and distress others.
- Children who are victimized become increasingly powerless; they find themselves trapped in relationships in which they are being abused.
- Children who are bystanders are also learning by example how to use power and aggression in relationships.

Bullying and power

Bullying is about power. Children learn that they can get power over others in many ways that we as adults might not even see. Power can come from an advantage in:

1 About bullying — basics	1	2 Why worry about bullying?	6	3 Bullying: myths, facts and solutions	10
4 Bullying in preschool	14	5 Elementary school children and bullying	19	6 Adolescents and bullying	25
7 Electronic bullying	30	8 Children who bully — what to do at home	36	9 What parents can do to help children who are victimized	40
10 How parents can work with the school	44	11 Bullying prevention through The Golden Rule	48	12 Resources for parents	52

- Size, age, strength, intelligence, athletic ability, etc.
- Social status with peers (e.g., more popular or dominant).
- Knowing that a child is vulnerable because he/she is overweight, has a learning disability or a mental health problem, etc.
- Being a member of a dominant group in society and using that power to bully someone because of his/her ethnicity or race, religion, gender, sexuality or sexual orientation, disability, financial disadvantage, etc.

The many types of bullying

Physical bullying involves physical aggression such as hitting, kicking, punching, or shoving someone, as well as destroying someone's belongings.

Verbal bullying occurs when children say hurtful things such as calling people names or laughing about weaknesses.

Social bullying occurs when children hurt another child's relationships by spreading hurtful rumors, excluding, ignoring, getting others not to be friends with this child, as well as when negative facial expressions and body language (e.g., eye rolling, turning a cold shoulder) are used.

Electronic or cyber bullying occurs when technology, such as a cell phone, social media such as Facebook or Twitter or the internet, is used to hurt someone. There are many ways to electronically bully others using text messages, social networking sites, e-mail, or the posting of embarrassing pictures or videos on the Internet.

1	About bullying — basics	1	2	Why worry about bullying?	6	3	Bullying: myths, facts and solutions	10
4	Bullying in preschool	14	5	Elementary school children and bullying	19	6	Adolescents and bullying	25
7	Electronic bullying	30	8	Children who bully — what to do at home	36	9	What parents can do to help children who are victimized	40
10	How parents can work with the school	44	11	Bullying prevention through The Golden Rule	48	12	Resources for parents	52

Bullying is a warm-up for long-term relationship problems

Bullying and victimization can start in early childhood and continue throughout the school years. Bullying is often worst when children move from elementary to middle school or from middle to high school. As children get older, physical bullying tends to decrease while verbal, social and electronic bullying increase.

The techniques of power and aggression learned in school playground bullying can transfer to sexual harassment, dating aggression and may even develop into workplace harassment, as well as marital, child, and elder abuse.

Boys' and girls' bullying

Both boys and girls can be involved in bullying others and both boys and girls can be victimized. Boys' bullying is more likely to involve physical aggression, whereas girls' bullying is more likely to involve social aggression and, therefore, may be more difficult to detect. Boys and girls are equally likely to be involved in verbal and electronic bullying.

How many children and youth are involved in bullying?

Bullying others: about 12% of children and teens report bullying others at least once in the last month.

Being bullied: about 22% of children and teens report being bullied by others at least once in the last month. The most common way

1	About bullying — basics	1	2 Why worry about bullying?	6	3	Bullying: myths, facts and solutions	10
4	Bullying in preschool	14	5 Elementary school children and bullying	19	6	Adolescents and bullying	25
7	Electronic bullying	30	8 Children who bully — what to do at home	36	9	What parents can do to help children who are victimized	40
10	How parents can work with the school	44	11 Bullying prevention through The Golden Rule	48	12	Resources for parents	52

these youth are victimized is verbally, followed by social bullying, then physical, and then electronically.

Bullying others and being victimized: About 40% of children and teens report engaging in both bullying and being victimized at least once in the last month. This is a problem because this significant percentage of children and young people are at risk for negative physical, emotional, and behavioral outcomes.

Where does bullying happen?

Bullying occurs anywhere that groups of children and teens are found. Children most often report that bullying takes place at school, especially in places where adults seldom supervise.

- In elementary school, bullying most often happens on the playground or in the washrooms.
- In high school, bullying most often happens in the hallways.
- Bullying also happens in classrooms when teachers are not watching.

Bullying also happens outside of school: on the way to or from school, in recreation settings and clubs, and during organized sports.

With cell phones and the Internet, children and teens are now being cyber bullied around the clock, in the safety of their own homes.

What parents can do

There are many things that parents can do to help prevent their children from being involved in bullying and to address their children's

1	About bullying — basics	1	2	Why worry about bullying?	6	3	Bullying: myths, facts and solutions	10
4	Bullying in preschool	14	5	Elementary school children and bullying	19	6	Adolescents and bullying	25
7	Electronic bullying	30	8	Children who bully — what to do at home	36	9	What parents can do to help children who are victimized	40
10	How parents can work with the school	44	11	Bullying prevention through The Golden Rule	48	12	Resources for parents	52

bullying issues when they do arise. These will vary depending on the child's age, the type of bullying and whether the child is bullying, being bullied or is a bystander. Steps that parents can take are discussed in detail in chapters 8 ("Children who bully – what to do at home"), 9 ("What parents can do to help children who are victimized") and 10 ("How parents can work with the school").

Used with permission.

1	About bullying — basics	1	2	Why worry about bullying?	6	3	Bullying: myths, facts and solutions	10
4	Bullying in preschool	14	5	Elementary school children and bullying	19	6	Adolescents and bullying	25
7	Electronic bullying	30	8	Children who bully — what to do at home	36	9	What parents can do to help children who are victimized	40
10	How parents can work with the school	44	11	Bullying prevention through The Golden Rule	48	12	Resources for parents	52

CHAPTER 2
Why worry about bullying?

Bullying is a problem that all parents should be aware of and concerned about because it touches most children and teens at some point in their school years and can have long-lasting impacts. Bullying affects all involved – those who bully, those who are bullied and those who are bystanders when bullying happens. (Note that we should avoid labeling children as "bullies" or "victims" because these labels limit thinking about the problem – bullying and being bullied arise less from any characteristics of a child and more from the child's social relationships.)

With support from parents, other adults and friends, most children and teens can change their relationships sufficiently so that they are able to cope with occasional involvement in bullying and not experience long-lasting impacts.

Why might my child be involved in bullying?

Bullying is a relationship problem. Children and teens can become involved in bullying for many reasons. There is no typical profile. It is important to recognize that children and teens learn their most important relationship lessons from the relationships they experience every day in their families.

Some youth might be victimized because:

- They are shy and withdrawn, so that aggressive youth know or believe that they are unlikely to report the bullying.

1 About bullying — basics	1	2 Why worry about bullying?	6	3 Bullying: myths, facts and solutions	10
4 Bullying in preschool	14	5 Elementary school children and bullying	19	6 Adolescents and bullying	25
7 Electronic bullying	30	8 Children who bully — what to do at home	36	9 What parents can do to help children who are victimized	40
10 How parents can work with the school	44	11 Bullying prevention through The Golden Rule	48	12 Resources for parents	52

- They have no friends and are excluded by a peer group. Children and teens who have at least one friend are less likely to be bullied than those with no friends.
- They are the object of jealousy and/or are bullied because of their positive characteristics.
- They have some characteristic that makes them different, such as a learning or physical disability, mental health problem, or difficulties managing their emotions or behavior.
- They feel a strong need to belong and have learned or believe that they will be included in a peer group if they endure bullying. This negative attention is better than being ignored and alone.
- They are just in the wrong place at the wrong time. By obtaining the details of a bullying incident, the parent can help the child recognize and avoid situations that are likely to be dangerous.

Some youth might bully others because:

- They have observed their parents and/or siblings using power and aggression to impose their will and get their way.
- They are socially skilled and have learned that bullying helps them gain power in the peer group and be popular.
- Those with poor social skills and few friends may bully to gain power and connect with peers, including becoming friends with peers who are aggressive.
- They have not learned the critical lessons of controlling their emotions and behavior. When they feel impulsive and explosive, some may bully others out of frustration.

1 About bullying — basics	1	2 Why worry about bullying?	6	3 Bullying: myths, facts and solutions	10
4 Bullying in preschool	14	5 Elementary school children and bullying	19	6 Adolescents and bullying	25
7 Electronic bullying	30	8 Children who bully — what to do at home	36	9 What parents can do to help children who are victimized	40
10 How parents can work with the school	44	11 Bullying prevention through The Golden Rule	48	12 Resources for parents	52

- Some youth join in bullying when their friends are doing it, because of a strong need to belong and a desire for acceptance by their friends.

Why worry about bullying – now and for the future?

- Bullying is a significant mental and physical health issue: involvement in bullying is linked with numerous health problems including anxiety, depression, and physical complaints, such as headaches and eating problems. These health problems arise for both youth who are victimized and those who bully.
- Involvement in bullying is related to poor grades or academic outcomes.
- Bullying is a warm-up for long-term relationship problems. Bullying and victimization can start in early childhood and continue through the school years. The lessons of power and aggression learned in playground bullying can transfer to sexual harassment, dating aggression and may extend to workplace harassment, as well as marital, child, and elder abuse.
- Relationship problems such as bullying are, as much as smoking, drinking or obesity, a contributor to early death.

Bullying is a relationship problem that requires relationship solutions

Relationship solutions, or making changes to relationships, is an approach to bullying that focuses on building children and teens'

1 About bullying — basics	1	2 Why worry about bullying?	6	3 Bullying: myths, facts and solutions	10
4 Bullying in preschool	14	5 Elementary school children and bullying	19	6 Adolescents and bullying	25
7 Electronic bullying	30	8 Children who bully — what to do at home	36	9 What parents can do to help children who are victimized	40
10 How parents can work with the school	44	11 Bullying prevention through The Golden Rule	48	12 Resources for parents	52

strengths while also identifying their challenges or the things that are difficult for them. The focus is on building up supportive relationships within their family, peer group, school, and broader community, since young people need consistent messages and responses to bullying across all of these settings.

To promote positive relationships, all children and teens involved in bullying incidents – those who bully, those who are victimized, as well as bystanders, must be included in efforts to stop bullying. None of these groups is immune to the negative effects of bullying. Since each child, whether bullying, bullied or bystander, deserves to grow up within healthy and respectful relationships, each of these groups must be included in efforts to reduce and stop bullying.

Used with permission.

1	About bullying — basics	1	2	Why worry about bullying?	6	3	Bullying: myths, facts and solutions	10
4	Bullying in preschool	14	5	Elementary school children and bullying	19	6	Adolescents and bullying	25
7	Electronic bullying	30	8	Children who bully — what to do at home	36	9	What parents can do to help children who are victimized	40
10	How parents can work with the school	44	11	Bullying prevention through The Golden Rule	48	12	Resources for parents	52

CHAPTER 3
Bullying: myths, facts and solutions

Myth #1: Children grow out of bullying.

Fact: Without intervention, a significant proportion of youth who bully others in childhood will continue to use their power negatively through adolescence and into adulthood. By identifying children who are experiencing problems early and intervening to help them, we can prevent patterns of aggression from becoming more and more established. Bullying at age 14 predicts future violent convictions, low job status, drug use and an unsuccessful life. Poor social relationships, as indicated by the presence of bullying behavior, are as big a contributor to early death as smoking, drinking and obesity.

Solution: Early identification and intervention of bullying. By making an early identification of children who are experiencing problems and intervening to help them, we can prevent patterns of aggressive interaction from becoming established in the child's or teen's behavior repertoire.

Myth #2: Only a small number of children have problems with bullying.

Fact: In North America, studies indicate that **more than 20% of students report being involved in bullying**. In an American study, 29% of students reported involvement in some aspect of bullying.* In Canadian data, 22% of youth report being bullied by others at least once in the past month. About 12% of youth report bullying others at least once in the past month. And about 40% of youth report

1	About bullying — basics	1	2	Why worry about bullying?	6	3	Bullying: myths, facts and solutions	10
4	Bullying in preschool	14	5	Elementary school children and bullying	19	6	Adolescents and bullying	25
7	Electronic bullying	30	8	Children who bully — what to do at home	36	9	What parents can do to help children who are victimized	40
10	How parents can work with the school	44	11	Bullying prevention through The Golden Rule	48	12	Resources for parents	52

engaging in both bullying and being victimized at least once in the past month. A bullying incident has been calculated to occur about once every 7½ minutes on the average school playground. This affects not just those being bullied or those bullying others. Even peers who are not involved but witness it – a common event given the incidence of bullying – report high levels of distress.

*U.S. National Institutes of Child Health and Development, April 24, 2001.

Solution: Given the widespread exposure of children to bullying, it is important to include all children in bullying prevention programs, regardless of the nature of their involvement in bullying. By making an early identification of children who are experiencing problems and intervening early to help them, we can prevent undesirable patterns from forming.

Myth #3: Reporting bullying will only make the problem worse.

Fact: It is incredibly difficult for children who are being victimized to remove themselves from this destructive relationship. However, simply by reporting their experience of victimization to one or more adults, these children experience significantly less victimization a year later. We have also learned that efforts by children to stop bullying on their own, without involving an adult, are usually unsuccessful and often lead to the bullying becoming worse. When no one talks about bullying, children who bully feel that they can carry on without any consequences. Silence and secrecy empower those who bully. Adult intervention can correct the power imbalance.

1	About bullying — basics	1	2	Why worry about bullying?	6	3	Bullying: myths, facts and solutions	10
4	Bullying in preschool	14	5	Elementary school children and bullying	19	6	Adolescents and bullying	25
7	Electronic bullying	30	8	Children who bully — what to do at home	36	9	What parents can do to help children who are victimized	40
10	How parents can work with the school	44	11	Bullying prevention through The Golden Rule	48	12	Resources for parents	52

Solution: Children need to be encouraged to report bullying and be given multiple ways of making these reports. Adults must convey the message that they want to know about children's experiences and that it is a job for adults to make the bullying stop.

Myth #4: Children who are victimized need to stand up and fight back.

Fact: Encouraging victimized children to fight back may, in fact, make the bullying interaction worse. We know that when children use aggressive ways of dealing with bullying situations, they tend to experience prolonged and more severe bullying interactions as a result.

Solution: Children should be encouraged to be assertive, but not aggressive, and to inform a trusted adult about what has happened to them.

Myth #5 : Bullying is a school problem.

Fact: Bullying occurs wherever children gather to live, learn, or play. As such, the majority of bullying tends to occur in the classroom, on the school playground, and on the school bus -- places where children are most often together. Although bullying tends to occur in school settings because of the way these settings bring children into a shared space for extended periods of time, we know that bullying is a community problem, not just a school problem.

Solution: Adults are essential for providing children and teens with examples of healthy relationships. All adults, not just parents and school teachers, are responsible for creating positive environments,

1	About bullying — basics	1	2	Why worry about bullying?	6	3	Bullying: myths, facts and solutions	10
4	Bullying in preschool	14	5	Elementary school children and bullying	19	6	Adolescents and bullying	25
7	Electronic bullying	30	8	Children who bully — what to do at home	36	9	What parents can do to help children who are victimized	40
10	How parents can work with the school	44	11	Bullying prevention through The Golden Rule	48	12	Resources for parents	52

promoting healthy relationships, and ending violence in the lives of children and teens. Adults are role models and must lead by example and refrain from using their power aggressively. Adults must look for, listen for, and respond to bullying. Together, adults can organize social activities in ways that protect and support children's relationships and stop bullying.

Myth #6: Bullying does not occur within the family or the family home.

Fact: Unfortunately, bullying does occur within families. Since bullying is a relationship problem in which there is repeated aggression by a person with greater power directed at a person with lesser power, it can and does occur in families. Repeated aggression within family relationships is most commonly called "abuse" or "family violence", and within peer relationships it is called "bullying" or "harassment". The family is the first context in which children learn about relationships, and lessons learned in the family provide the example and foundation for future relationships.

Solution: It is critically important that children experience secure and healthy relationships in the family. There is of course a power imbalance between parent and child, but relationships in which there is a power imbalance are precisely the relationships in which the person with more power has the responsibility to safeguard the well-being of the more vulnerable person. **Through providing a model of respectful relationships** and taking responsibility for the well-being of those who are dependent and vulnerable, both within and beyond the family, adults can help to promote healthy relationships and prevent bullying and abuse.

1	About bullying — basics	1	2	Why worry about bullying?	6	3	Bullying: myths, facts and solutions	10
4	Bullying in preschool	14	5	Elementary school children and bullying	19	6	Adolescents and bullying	25
7	Electronic bullying	30	8	Children who bully — what to do at home	36	9	What parents can do to help children who are victimized	40
10	How parents can work with the school	44	11	Bullying prevention through The Golden Rule	48	12	Resources for parents	52

CHAPTER 4
Bullying in preschool

Recognizing bullying

Because of the innocence of preschool children, many people are surprised that bullying occurs during this age period. Of course, preschoolers fight with their siblings and friends, but when does it become bullying? Younger preschoolers often don't hide their bullying behavior until they mature enough to understand that it is not OK. **That's why the preschool period is an important time for bullying prevention, because adults have more opportunities to see and address bullying episodes.**

Preschool bullying takes the following forms:

- **Physical:** hitting, kicking, biting, destroying what others have made, and taking toys. etc.

- **Verbal bullying:** name calling ("cry baby"), mocking, hurtful teasing, threatening, etc.

- **Social bullying:** excluding others from the group ("you can't play with us"), friendship withdrawal ("I won't be your friend anymore"), or damaging friendships ("I'm going to tell Ashley not to invite you to her party").

When to worry if bullying is a problem

The years from two to six are a time of amazing transformation; the curious, impulsive, and socially naïve toddler becomes the sophisticated six-year-old ready to work and play alongside classmates,

1	About bullying — basics	1	2	Why worry about bullying?	6	3	Bullying: myths, facts and solutions	10
4	Bullying in preschool	14	5	Elementary school children and bullying	19	6	Adolescents and bullying	25
7	Electronic bullying	30	8	Children who bully — what to do at home	36	9	What parents can do to help children who are victimized	40
10	How parents can work with the school	44	11	Bullying prevention through The Golden Rule	48	12	Resources for parents	52

follow classroom rules, and form enduring friendships. There will be missteps for all children during this transformation. Although preschoolers can pick up on the emotions of others, they tend to see the world from their own point of view, especially when they are feeling hurt. It is hard for them to take the perspective of others. Parents and caregivers should not be discouraged when preschoolers get involved in peer conflicts, including bullying, but should play an active role in setting limits on hurtful behavior, and teach, reward and provide a model of respectful and caring behaviors.

Many preschoolers have relatively short-term (less than three months) episodes of bullying, and with extra adult support and coaching, the problem is usually resolved. It is rare for a preschooler to show an enduring pattern of involvement in bullying.

Signs that your child may be bullied include:
- being afraid to go to daycare/pre-school
- appearing isolated from the peer group
- exhibiting anxious or fearful behavior
- complaining of feeling sick
- being unhappy or irritable
- having trouble sleeping

Signs that your child may be bullying others include:
- being aggressive with other children or animals
- bossy and dominant behaviors

1 About bullying — basics	1	2 Why worry about bullying?	6	3 Bullying: myths, facts and solutions	10
4 Bullying in preschool	14	5 Elementary school children and bullying	19	6 Adolescents and bullying	25
7 Electronic bullying	30	8 Children who bully — what to do at home	36	9 What parents can do to help children who are victimized	40
10 How parents can work with the school	44	11 Bullying prevention through The Golden Rule	48	12 Resources for parents	52

- not following rules or cooperating with parents and/or teachers
- appearing easily frustrated, or quick to anger
- failing to recognize the impact of his/her behavior
- understanding but not caring about the impact of his/her behavior

If you see these signs and feel concerned, talk with your child's teachers and caregivers. Ask them to observe your child when playing with peers. Ensure that all of the responsible adults increase their moment-to-moment coaching, and send consistent messages.

The degree of support a child gets is critical, because a child cannot be expected to change if the environment doesn't actively support healthy peer relationships. If this is the case, consider finding a more responsive caregiver, childcare, or preschool for your child.

If your preschooler is repeatedly bullying others

There can be many reasons for bullying others. Identifying the reasons will help you choose a course of action.

- Reflect on your preschooler's relationships in the family, and ask yourself if the child is experiencing painful feelings in these relationships. Some children try to "get rid" of these painful feelings by inflicting them upon siblings or peers. Some children act out the behavior they see modeled by parents or siblings. If you believe that there are relationship issues in your family, address them.

1	About bullying — basics	1	2	Why worry about bullying?	6	3	Bullying: myths, facts and solutions	10
4	Bullying in preschool	14	5	Elementary school children and bullying	19	6	Adolescents and bullying	25
7	Electronic bullying	30	8	Children who bully — what to do at home	36	9	What parents can do to help children who are victimized	40
10	How parents can work with the school	44	11	Bullying prevention through The Golden Rule	48	12	Resources for parents	52

- Other preschoolers have an explosive and impulsive temperament, and their bullying behavior reflects a delay in self-regulation skills which they should have developed at their age.
- Other preschoolers bully because it is rewarding – they get attention from peers and/or material things from bullying.

A pattern of aggressive behavior developed in early childhood can be long-lasting, so address it early.

If your preschooler is repeatedly victimized by peers

There are many reasons why some preschoolers are victimized.

- Some are shy and socially anxious, so that they do not defend themselves or tell adults what is happening. Other children learn that they can get away with bullying them.
- Some preschoolers may be impulsive and very active, and may unintentionally bother other children, who then retaliate.
- Preschoolers who have delays in language, motor or social skills are vulnerable to victimization in environments with low levels of adult supervision.

Children who are often bullied need adults to protect them and **to connect them to other caring, friendly children**. Adults should foster these connections through selecting partners and making seating or group assignments. Parents can invite caring children over for play dates, and remain involved to structure the activities, coaching the preschoolers through rough spots. **Teach the child to hold his or her head high, look directly at the other child and say "That hurts my feelings." "That is not fair." "If you don't stop, I will tell the teacher."**

1	About bullying — basics	1	2	Why worry about bullying?	6	3	Bullying: myths, facts and solutions	10
4	Bullying in preschool	14	5	Elementary school children and bullying	19	6	Adolescents and bullying	25
7	Electronic bullying	30	8	Children who bully — what to do at home	36	9	What parents can do to help children who are victimized	40
10	How parents can work with the school	44	11	Bullying prevention through The Golden Rule	48	12	Resources for parents	52

If the problem persists, get some help for you and your child. You could ask your child's school or your family doctor for a referral to a child and family service, a psychologist, or other professional. You might also enroll in parenting classes to learn what supports children need from their parents to develop in the healthiest way. *Parenting is the hardest job – we all need help along the way!*

Resolving bullying problems

Birthday-party attendance leads to problems on the playground

Rebecca was a spirited 5½ year-old who often got into conflicts with the little girls at her preschool. When she was "on the outs" with the girls, she would play with Timothy, a younger boy who was happy to do whatever she wanted. Rebecca was one of the four guests invited to Timothy's fourth birthday party at his home. Rebecca was older and more socially savvy than Timothy, and very much enjoyed her status as honored guest at the party. The morning after the birthday party, Timothy arrived at preschool and spotted Rebecca and some of her friends sitting on top of a climber. He began to climb up to join them. Looking down, Rebecca said "You can't climb up here, you are still a baby. And I am never coming to your house again." Timothy was stung by her words, and his eyes filled up with tears.

The preschool teacher was standing nearby and observed what happened. Her goals for intervening in-the-moment were to provide support to Timothy, and teach Rebecca that her behavior was not acceptable. The teacher gave Timothy a hug, and said "I heard the hurtful words that Rebecca said to you." Then looking up at Rebecca, the teacher said, "Rebecca, please remember that everyone is allowed to use this climber. What feeling do you see when you look at Timothy's face?" Rebecca did not answer immediately, but her discomfort was clear. After a pause Rebecca said, "I'm sorry, Timothy." The teacher replied, "I am glad you said you were sorry, because your words hurt his feelings." Later that day, the preschool teacher reviewed "caring words" and " hurtful words" with the entire class, and reinforced the message that everyone in the class is expected to be caring.

---

1 About bullying — basics **1**	2 Why worry about bullying? **6**	3 Bullying: myths, facts and solutions **10**
4 Bullying in preschool **14**	5 Elementary school children and bullying **19**	6 Adolescents and bullying **25**
7 Electronic bullying **30**	8 Children who bully — what to do at home **36**	9 What parents can do to help children who are victimized **40**
10 How parents can work with the school **44**	11 Bullying prevention through The Golden Rule **48**	12 Resources for parents **52**

CHAPTER 5
Elementary school children and bullying

Bullying among elementary school children brings new challenges. New forms of bullying emerge. Children are more reluctant to report bullying episodes, and bullying is most likely to occur where adults are not present. And the peer group plays a more important role in encouraging or discouraging bullying than in pre-school.

Recognizing bullying

Bullying among elementary school children **may be more difficult to detect because they often use covert forms of aggression such as social and electronic bullying.** Incidents of physical bullying may occur less often than in preschool. In some cases, the distress of the victimized child may be the only indicator that bullying has occurred.

Some common examples of behaviors used to bully in elementary school are name-calling, pushing, giggling or making faces when another child talks, excluding from a game, ignoring, tattling to get a child in trouble, using a child's name as an insult, making a point not to sit or line up near a certain child, or writing negative messages on the internet.

Bullying can happen between siblings or friends when one child continually exerts power over the other, causing distress to the victimized child.

When to worry if bullying is a problem

Bullying is always a problem that requires immediate intervention. To assess the severity of the problem, ask your child these four

1	About bullying — basics	1	2	Why worry about bullying?	6	3	Bullying: myths, facts and solutions	10
4	Bullying in preschool	14	5	Elementary school children and bullying	19	6	Adolescents and bullying	25
7	Electronic bullying	30	8	Children who bully — what to do at home	36	9	What parents can do to help children who are victimized	40
10	How parents can work with the school	44	11	Bullying prevention through The Golden Rule	48	12	Resources for parents	52

questions: How often does it happen? How long has it been going on? In how many places does it occur and how has it affected you?

Signs your child is being bullied:

- acting differently than he or she normally does
- being afraid of going to school
- complaining of physical ailments (stomach aches, trouble sleeping)
- appearing worried, unhappy, moody
- showing decreased interest in previously enjoyed activities
- demonstrating low self-esteem
- threatening to hurt him or herself
- appearing to have missing or damaged items
- having unexplained injuries
- complaining of being left out of activities or the peer group
- losing interest in visiting or talking with friends
- appearing distressed when online

By identifying the signs of involvement in bullying, parents can stop bullying behaviors and help their children develop healthy relationships with their peers.

Signs your child may be bullying others include:

- being aggressive with children, adults, pets

1 About bullying — basics	1	2 Why worry about bullying?	6	3 Bullying: myths, facts and solutions	10
4 Bullying in preschool	14	5 Elementary school children and bullying	19	6 Adolescents and bullying	25
7 Electronic bullying	30	8 Children who bully — what to do at home	36	9 What parents can do to help children who are victimized	40
10 How parents can work with the school	44	11 Bullying prevention through The Golden Rule	48	12 Resources for parents	52

- holding a positive view of aggression or passing off teasing as a joke
- being easily frustrated and/or quick to anger
- demonstrating bossy and manipulative behavior
- leaving people out intentionally
- having aggressive friends
- demonstrating difficulty resisting peer pressure
- appearing to not recognize or care about others' feelings or the impact of his/her behavior on others (e.g., laughs, blames the victimized child)
- having unexplained objects or money
- being secretive about online activities and switching screens or programs when others walk by

How to help your child if he/she is being bullied

- Thank your child for being brave enough to come forward.
- Tell the child the bullying is not their fault.
- Acknowledge the seriousness. Track and keep a record of details of the bullying incident(s).
- Tell your child to report bullying to you until it has completely stopped.
- Explain that telling/reporting is to get someone out of trouble and is different from tattling/ratting to get someone into trouble.

1	About bullying — basics	1	2	Why worry about bullying?	6	3	Bullying: myths, facts and solutions	10
4	Bullying in preschool	14	5	Elementary school children and bullying	19	6	Adolescents and bullying	25
7	Electronic bullying	30	8	Children who bully — what to do at home	36	9	What parents can do to help children who are victimized	40
10	How parents can work with the school	44	11	Bullying prevention through The Golden Rule	48	12	Resources for parents	52

- Practice with your child what to say and do in a bullying situation:
  - confidently tell the child who is bullying to STOP!
  - Walk away and report it to your mom or dad if you are at home and, if it happens at school, report it to your homeroom teacher or another trusted adult.
- Make a Safety Plan.
  - Tell your child to stick to areas where adults are present.
  - Make sure your child can walk home with someone.
- Take action on your child's behalf by reporting the bullying suffered by your child to the other significant adults in your child's life, such as home-room teacher, the coach for a sport that the child is involved in and any other adults who have regular contact with the child and take an interest in the child's well-being.
- Have your child join a sport, lesson, or club outside of school to help create friendship opportunities, reduce stress, and acquire new skills and self-esteem.
- Follow up. Your child may not tell you if bullying continues.

When telling the child to be assertive in standing up for herself/himself, be sure to tell your child **not to act aggressively** by physically or verbally attacking the child is who is bullying, since this can make things worse.

How to help your child if he/she bullies others

- Establish what is acceptable behavior.
- Coach your child on how to ask for things and express feelings without bullying.

#	Topic	Page	#	Topic	Page	#	Topic	Page
1	About bullying — basics	1	2	Why worry about bullying?	6	3	Bullying: myths, facts and solutions	10
4	Bullying in preschool	14	5	Elementary school children and bullying	19	6	Adolescents and bullying	25
7	Electronic bullying	30	8	Children who bully — what to do at home	36	9	What parents can do to help children who are victimized	40
10	How parents can work with the school	44	11	Bullying prevention through The Golden Rule	48	12	Resources for parents	52

- Supervise your child's play with other children.
- Be consistent in applying consequences by replacing privileges with activities that develop relationship skills, for example doing, making or building something together with other children.
- To encourage empathy, teach your child how to identify the emotions of victimized characters using books or movies. Ask your child how he/she thinks a victimized character feels.
- To make amends, encourage your child to make an apology and/or restore damaged items.
- To help your child use power positively, give opportunities to highlight any special skills that the child has. The positive feedback will show the child that their abilities are valued and will lead the child to spend more energy on those abilities.
- Praise your child for being cooperative as he/she learns.
- Follow up to monitor progress.

Reaching out for help

Bullying is best addressed through the combined efforts of parents, teachers and the community.

- Make other adults who are important to the child aware of the bullying and its seriousness by communicating regularly.
- Find out what school and community supports exist for children involved in bullying. Speak up for appropriate supervision and for tracking of incidents so that principals or activity leaders will know which children and teens need help.

1	About bullying — basics	1	2	Why worry about bullying?	6	3	Bullying: myths, facts and solutions	10
4	Bullying in preschool	14	5	Elementary school children and bullying	19	6	Adolescents and bullying	25
7	Electronic bullying	30	8	Children who bully — what to do at home	36	9	What parents can do to help children who are victimized	40
10	How parents can work with the school	44	11	Bullying prevention through The Golden Rule	48	12	Resources for parents	52

Resolving bullying problems

Shy boy goes out for the elementary baseball team

Peter was a shy, studious boy who was more comfortable with adults than with peers. He loved sports of all kinds, and his parents encouraged him to try out for the baseball team to help him make friends. After he attended his first try-out for the school baseball team, two boys taunted him and called him names in the locker room. One of these boys had been verbally bullying him on-and-off for several years, and though this had bothered Peter he'd ignored it and hadn't told anyone. This time was different and much worse – the taunting occurred in front of an audience, and many of the boys laughed. Peter was nervous about attending the next week's try-out but he did anyway and played well. He remained on the field chatting with the coach quite late, hoping to be alone in the locker room. As he was changing, the boys who bullied him before appeared. The bigger boy poked his stomach with a baseball bat and called him a "fat fag" repeatedly. Peter appeared very distraught when his father picked him up, and told his father what happened in the car.

Peter's father reported the two locker room incidents to the school principal. Both the coach and the principal met with Peter and assured him that they would make sure he felt safe so he could play baseball on the team. Peter's parents practiced assertive responses he could use if anyone bullied him again. The boys who had been bullying him met with the coach and the principal. Initially they claimed to have all been just joking around, but they got the message that the behavior was unacceptable and the use of the baseball bat made it a serious offence. Their parents were notified. One of the mothers confided to the principal that she was overwhelmed by her son's aggression at home. With the principal's support, the family was referred to a local agency for counseling. The parents of the other boy were initially defensive and denied their son would intentionally do such a thing. Because the principal maintained a nonjudgmental and problem-solving attitude, the parents understood that this was an opportunity for an important life lesson. The two boys were required to read a book about bullying with their parents, and then to give a presentation about what they learned to younger students. They were also told that the coach would be checking in with Peter consistently for the next several weeks, and if there were more incidents they would not be allowed to play baseball on the team.

1	About bullying — basics	1	2	Why worry about bullying?	6	3	Bullying: myths, facts and solutions	10
4	Bullying in preschool	14	5	Elementary school children and bullying	19	6	Adolescents and bullying	25
7	Electronic bullying	30	8	Children who bully — what to do at home	36	9	What parents can do to help children who are victimized	40
10	How parents can work with the school	44	11	Bullying prevention through The Golden Rule	48	12	Resources for parents	52

CHAPTER 6
Adolescents and bullying

Adolescent bullying takes place in the context of a challenging period of life for many individuals who bully or are bullied. Hormonal changes, school pressures, the development of romantic relationships and/or peer pressure make adolescents more susceptible to involvement in bullying. These challenges also make adolescents more vulnerable to the detrimental and long term effects of bullying. The social interactions among adolescents become more sophisticated as they develop social skills, but can also lead to an increased awareness of others' vulnerabilities, and of the effects of power imbalances in relationships. As a consequence, adolescents engage in a wide variety of bullying behaviors including verbal, social, and electronic, along with sexual harassment and dating aggression. Sexual harassment includes any unwanted comments, inappropriate gestures or behaviors about sex or gender. Dating aggression involves any intentional sexual, physical, or psychological attack that occurs in a dating relationship.

Because of physical maturation, adolescents also have an increased awareness of sexuality and sexual identity, which can become a focus for bullying.

When to worry if bullying is a problem

During transitions from middle to high school, bullying tends to peak. Given the higher risk of being bullied, and the increased vulnerability of adolescents, it is important for parents to stay alert for signs of bullying and/or sexual harassment.

1	About bullying — basics	1	2	Why worry about bullying?	6	3	Bullying: myths, facts and solutions	10
4	Bullying in preschool	14	5	Elementary school children and bullying	19	6	Adolescents and bullying	25
7	Electronic bullying	30	8	Children who bully — what to do at home	36	9	What parents can do to help children who are victimized	40
10	How parents can work with the school	44	11	Bullying prevention through The Golden Rule	48	12	Resources for parents	52

Signs that your child may be bullied include:
- avoiding going to school
- loss of interest in activities
- anxiousness, fear and low self-esteem
- complaints of feeling unwell, including trouble sleeping
- general unhappiness and/or irritability
- isolation from the peer group
- threats to hurt themselves or others
- losing things, needing money and/or having damaged clothing or belongings
- changes in performance at school

Signs your adolescent may be bullying others include:
- low concern for others' feelings
- bossiness, manipulation and frustration
- quickness to anger
- positive views of aggression
- not recognizing the impact of behaviors
- having friends who bully or are aggressive
- having trouble standing up to peer pressure
- unexplained money or possessions, or being secretive about these things

#	Section	Page	#	Section	Page	#	Section	Page
1	About bullying — basics	1	2	Why worry about bullying?	6	3	Bullying: myths, facts and solutions	10
4	Bullying in preschool	14	5	Elementary school children and bullying	19	6	Adolescents and bullying	25
7	Electronic bullying	30	8	Children who bully — what to do at home	36	9	What parents can do to help children who are victimized	40
10	How parents can work with the school	44	11	Bullying prevention through The Golden Rule	48	12	Resources for parents	52

How to help your adolescent if he/she is bullied

- Listen, be supportive, express concern, and thank him/her for being brave enough to come forward.

- Work together to create solutions to the problem by teaching assertiveness, by encouraging your teen to as much as possible avoid areas where bullying happens, and by encouraging your teen to pursue other activities which can help improve self-confidence and a sense of value and worth. Ask your teen what kind of support from you might be helpful.

- Teach assertiveness by getting your teen to practice holding his/her head up and making eye contact.

- Encourage your teen to avoid areas where bullying happens, to ignore the people who bully, and to stay close to others who will stick up for him/her.

- Teach your child to be assertive by standing up for him/herself if being treated unfairly or aggressively. At the same time, remind your teen or child not to respond aggressively, as in physically or verbally attacking the person who is acting badly. Responding with aggressive behavior has a good chance of making the problem worse.

It is important for parents to convey that they are willing to do whatever it takes to help, and it is critical to keep talking to teens! Encourage them to come to you or to speak to other trusted adults to monitor bullying.

How to help your adolescent if he/she bullies others

- Provide a good example of positive relationships in the way that the parent treats the teen and other children with warmth and respect, and in what the teen sees and hears of the parent's behavior in dealing with the parent's social world.

- Talk to your teen about diversity and acceptance in order to teach him/her that being different does not mean others do not deserve respect.
- Teach your child to see people as individuals, not stereotypes or categories.
- Encourage your teen to put him/herself in the other person's shoes and to think of what it feels like to be beaten up, threatened or excluded.
- Work with your teen to come up with alternative ways to resolve conflict.
- Encourage your teen to do what's right, to hang out with friends who influence in a positive rather than negative way.
- Keep the lines of communication open by listening without judging and remaining calm.
- Be a role model. How you deal with conflict and frustration in your home will influence how your teenager will handle these challenges with others.

Ensure your teen knows what constitutes bullying, sexual harassment and dating aggression, and that these behaviors are not acceptable to you, to the teachers or coaches whom your teen admires or for that matter to people who many teens look up to as an inspiration or a role model, such as Lady Gaga.

Reaching out for help

As difficult as it is for you to learn that your teen is involved in bullying, remember that it is an even more difficult issue for your teen

#	Topic	Page	#	Topic	Page	#	Topic	Page
1	About bullying — basics	1	2	Why worry about bullying?	6	3	Bullying: myths, facts and solutions	10
4	Bullying in preschool	14	5	Elementary school children and bullying	19	6	Adolescents and bullying	25
7	Electronic bullying	30	8	Children who bully — what to do at home	36	9	What parents can do to help children who are victimized	40
10	How parents can work with the school	44	11	Bullying prevention through The Golden Rule	48	12	Resources for parents	52

who is struggling to define who he/she is and how to behave. Speak up on behalf of your teen, and take actions to help resolve the problem. Make connections with significant adults in your teen's life (e.g., teachers, coaches, other parents) to make them aware of the problem and to develop steps to ensure the bullying stops. Consult with school and community resources on bullying and sexual harassment. If there is suspected sexual aggression or abuse, it may be necessary to contact police or child protection services.

Both teens who bully others and those who are bullied require support to address their relationship problems. By identifying the signs of involvement in bullying, parents can support their children and teens before the problem becomes extremely serious. If a bullying problem persists, get some help for your teen. You could ask your teen's school or family doctor for a referral to an adolescent and family service, a psychologist, or other professional. Because relationships with peers are so important in adolescence, problems such as bullying can lead to mental health problems, which are best dealt with as soon as they arise.

Used with permission.

1	About bullying — basics	1	2	Why worry about bullying?	6	3	Bullying: myths, facts and solutions	10
4	Bullying in preschool	14	5	Elementary school children and bullying	19	6	Adolescents and bullying	25
7	Electronic bullying	30	8	Children who bully — what to do at home	36	9	What parents can do to help children who are victimized	40
10	How parents can work with the school	44	11	Bullying prevention through The Golden Rule	48	12	Resources for parents	52

CHAPTER 7
Electronic bullying

Electronic bullying or cyberbullying refers to repeated harm inflicted through electronic media. It includes the use of electronic devices such as cell phones or the Internet to threaten, harass, embarrass, socially exclude, or damage others' reputations and friendships. Electronic bullying includes bullying that may occur through any kind of electronic communication, such as text messaging, e-mail, electronic photos, videos, on-line chat rooms, or websites.

Electronic bullying presents many unique challenges. Electronic bullying can be anonymous. That is, perpetrators can hide behind screen names or e-mail addresses so that their identity is not readily identifiable. **Because of this perceived anonymity, electronic bullying can be especially harsh.**

Another challenge is that electronic bullying is often disseminated to a wide audience. With just a few clicks, a child or teen can send emails making fun of someone to their entire class or school, or post them to a website for the whole world to see—with devastating speed. Also, once electronic information is posted or sent, it can be more or less impossible to eliminate. Consequently, **children who are victimized by electronic bullying often perceive it as inescapable.** And because electronic bullying can reach the person being bullied anywhere, even in that person's home, it threatens them in the place they most need to feel safe.

When to Worry About Electronic Bullying

Electronic bullying is extremely difficult to monitor as adults are often unable to detect inappropriate technology use. Furthermore,

1	About bullying — basics	1	2	Why worry about bullying?	6	3	Bullying: myths, facts and solutions	10
4	Bullying in preschool	14	5	Elementary school children and bullying	19	6	Adolescents and bullying	25
7	Electronic bullying	30	8	Children who bully — what to do at home	36	9	What parents can do to help children who are victimized	40
10	How parents can work with the school	44	11	Bullying prevention through The Golden Rule	48	12	Resources for parents	52

youth are afraid to report electronic bullying for fear of having their online or electronic communication privileges taken away from them as a consequence. It is important to assure them they will not necessarily happen -- it depends on how the situation is resolved.

Signs your child is being bullied electronically:

- appearing distressed when online or while using a cell phone
- secrecy about online activities, hiding or switching screens when others walk by
- avoiding discussing online activities
- changes in pattern of computer or cell phone usage

Signs your child may be electronically bullying others:

- secrecy about online activities, hiding or switching screens when others walk by
- spending longer than usual hours online
- becoming upset if not allowed to use the computer, or using multiple online accounts.

These behaviors and emotions in your child may indicate that bullying is a problem.

How to help your child if he or she is being electronically bullied

- **Be ready to listen.** Thank him/her for being brave and coming forward. Explain that it is his/her right to feel safe online. Ask

1	About bullying — basics	1	2	Why worry about bullying?	6	3	Bullying: myths, facts and solutions	10
4	Bullying in preschool	14	5	Elementary school children and bullying	19	6	Adolescents and bullying	25
7	Electronic bullying	30	8	Children who bully — what to do at home	36	9	What parents can do to help children who are victimized	40
10	How parents can work with the school	44	11	Bullying prevention through The Golden Rule	48	12	Resources for parents	52

for details, and convey your concern about all reports, even seemingly trivial ones. Let your child know you are there to support him/her.

- **Be your child's advocate – act and speak up for him/her**
- Once your child has come forward, it's your turn to act. Consider setting up new accounts for your child.
- **Find out what happened and whether it has stopped.** Keep a record of what occurred—print the e-mails, chat room history, or web posting, or save the phone message.
- **Report electronic bullying** to the school and to your internet service provider, and in extreme cases, to the police.
- **Encourage your child not to reply to hurtful messages**. Responding may exacerbate the situation.
- **Encourage your child to talk** to you about any continuing problems with electronic bullying.
- **Recharge all of your child's electronics in your bedroom at night**

If your child bullies others electronically

- Be clear that electronic bullying is not acceptable behavior.
- Encourage empathy. Because electronic bullying is usually anonymous, a child or teen who bullies may not realize the harm their actions cause. Talk with your child about acceptable behavior, both on and offline. Encourage thinking about how it feels to be bullied electronically. Emphasize the loss of safety the bullying produces and the feeling of helplessness. Help your child understand that what may seem like fun can cause harm to another individual.

1	About bullying — basics	1	2	Why worry about bullying?	6	3	Bullying: myths, facts and solutions	10
4	Bullying in preschool	14	5	Elementary school children and bullying	19	6	Adolescents and bullying	25
7	Electronic bullying	30	8	Children who bully — what to do at home	36	9	What parents can do to help children who are victimized	40
10	How parents can work with the school	44	11	Bullying prevention through The Golden Rule	48	12	Resources for parents	52

- Ask your child to promise to stop his or her bullying activity. Emphasize the serious consequences that can arise for your child by continuing bullying, such as problems with friends at school, loss of certain privileges at home or even legal consequences.

- Encourage your child to apologize to the people he/she has hurt online.

- To prevent future occurrences, keep the computer in a common area so you can monitor your child's online activities.

- If the child refuses to agree to stop bullying activities, the parent should let the child know that the consequence will be the removal of all online and phone privileges until the child does agree.

Preventing electronic bullying before it happens

- **Learn about online activities.** Many parents lack the computer savvy to effectively supervise their children's media use. Take the time to familiarize yourself with technology and online spaces. Learn the email, chat, instant-messaging (IM), blogs, and websites that your children use. You will be better prepared to help deal with electronic bullying if you are aware of social conventions such as acronyms and emoticons.

- **Monitor computer use.** Keep the computer in a common area so you can monitor activities and your child's reactions to online communications. Be aware of your children's emotions and check in with them if they appear distressed. Have clearly defined family rules about your access to your child's electronic communications.

- **Encourage your child to unplug.** Despite the importance of online interactions among teens, parents should encourage kids to limit their time online. Fostering friendships offline reduces the risk of electronic bullying and provides a source of support.

1	About bullying — basics	1	2	Why worry about bullying?	6	3	Bullying: myths, facts and solutions	10
4	Bullying in preschool	14	5	Elementary school children and bullying	19	6	Adolescents and bullying	25
7	Electronic bullying	30	8	Children who bully — what to do at home	36	9	What parents can do to help children who are victimized	40
10	How parents can work with the school	44	11	Bullying prevention through The Golden Rule	48	12	Resources for parents	52

- **Start talking about electronic bullying.** Your children may be hesitant to approach you about electronic bullying because they fear losing their computer privileges; assure him/her that this will not happen if the bullying problem can be resolved. It is up to you to start this conversation if you have reason to think that something may be wrong.

Discuss healthy relationships, both on and offline, with your child. Assure him or her that you are there to offer support if there is a problem. That is, listen to what they are saying without judging and try to understand their perspective. You want to create an openness in the communication that will enable your child to come and talk to you with his or her concerns.

Resolving bullying problems

Sleepover leads to electronic bullying

Four months into High School, Susan attended a sleep-over with five other girls. Susan was thrilled to be invited to this party, because she really wanted to be a part of such a popular group. At the party the girls put on their sleep wear then did each other's hair and make-up, then vamped it up for the camera. The following Monday at school, a girl who had not attended the party asked Susan if she had seen the website, "Hot Bods" that showed pictures from the sleepover. As soon as she could Susan went online, and to her profound embarrassment she saw a picture of herself wearing a tee shirt and underwear – under which was the caption, "Definitely doesn't belong!" Below that were several negative comments about her body.

Aside from feeling like the whole school was laughing at her, the words "doesn't belong" really hurt. Susan told no one but over the next few days she kept to herself at school and was irritable at home. The next weekend when her mother asked her if she had any plans Susan burst into tears, saying " I have no plans and I never will, because I have no friends". Slowly, her mother got the story out of her, and Susan showed her the website. Her mother was not only horrified for her daughter, she was also concerned that the girls had posted such inappropriate pictures on line. Although Susan begged her mom not to notify the school principal, Susan's mother was adamant that this was the right thing to do, and reminded Susan of the school's Code of Conduct that they had both signed at the beginning of the year.

continued on next page 35

1	About bullying — basics	1	2	Why worry about bullying?	6	3	Bullying: myths, facts and solutions	10
4	Bullying in preschool	14	5	Elementary school children and bullying	19	6	Adolescents and bullying	25
7	Electronic bullying	30	8	Children who bully — what to do at home	36	9	What parents can do to help children who are victimized	40
10	How parents can work with the school	44	11	Bullying prevention through The Golden Rule	48	12	Resources for parents	52

Resolving bullying problems

continued from page 34

The following Monday, Susan's mother got in touch with the principal of Susan's school and gave him the URL for the website. Because electronic bullying affects the social climate at school, it was the School Board's policy for the principal to address the issue. A school social worker was brought in to provide counseling to Susan and her parents. Her parents understood the need to reassure Susan that she had not done anything wrong and that her right to privacy and respect was violated. The offensive web site was investigated by the School Board's Internet Technology Department, and the source of the website was quickly identified and the website was removed. The principal notified all the parents of the girls who attended the party. The principal and a guidance counselor met with each of the girls. There were two objectives for this meeting: to help the girls understand the negative impact of their action on Susan, and to help them appreciate the need for internet safety. Each student was assigned to write a research project about electronic bullying and a personal reflection about their role in the incident. Although each girl sent Susan a letter of apology, Susan decided not to pursue the friendship with any of them. The principal also implemented a school-wide initiative to educate all the students about appropriate internet behavior and online safety without mentioning the specific incident. Many students took it upon themselves to reach out to Susan, and their expressions of care and concern were very helpful to Susan's healing.

Used with permission.

1	About bullying — basics	1	2	Why worry about bullying?	6	3	Bullying: myths, facts and solutions	10
4	Bullying in preschool	14	5	Elementary school children and bullying	19	6	Adolescents and bullying	25
7	Electronic bullying	30	8	Children who bully — what to do at home	36	9	What parents can do to help children who are victimized	40
10	How parents can work with the school	44	11	Bullying prevention through The Golden Rule	48	12	Resources for parents	52

CHAPTER 8
Children who bully — what to do at home

If you find out that your child or teen is bullying others, there are several things that you can do as a parent to help repair the situation and decrease the likelihood of future bullying.

Taking responsibility and repairing

Once you learn that your child is bullying others, you must deliver a consistent message that bullying is not acceptable. Educational consequences are an important component of supporting this message and offer an opportunity to help children understand the effects of bullying. For example, an appropriate consequence if you learn your child has bullied, is to have him or her stay in for the weekend and write a letter of apology, and write (or draw) what it feels like to be bullied. This consequence focuses on teaching children empathy skills, which is an area that is less well developed in children and teens who bully.

Through conversations about stories in books, television and movies, help your chlld learn words and feelings that put him or her in the shoes of the victimized child and let your child think about what it would be like to be picked on, put down or left out. You can also model empathy by sharing your own feelings in bullying situations and explaining in age-appropriate language why you feel the way you do. The goal in teaching empathy is to help your child to take on the other person's perspective before they act.

Once time has been given to consequences and empathy, it is important to teach the process of repairing the relationship with the child who has been bullied. Teaching your child to actively seek to repair the relationship is important as it makes the child take responsibility for his or her actions. Ensure that this repair process is carried out in a genuine manner which enhances both parties' feeling of self-worth.

Teaching positive ways to deal with anger

In addition to lacking empathy, children who bully are often unskilled in managing difficult emotions such as anger and frustration. Parents can help their children identify these feelings, as a first step in dealing with them in a more aware and socially harmonious way. When a child is getting angry, ask the child how he/she feels/and how his/her body feels. Also, help the child focus on behavioral strategies to calm him/herself. The simplest of these is to learn to take a Time Out. As a parent, it is important to be ready to respond to moment-to-moment opportunities for coaching and support.

Helping children to communicate what they want or need is essential to managing frustration or angry feelings. It is helpful to provide specific examples of words they should use to ask for what they need or want. Acting out these scenarios allows children to practice in safe environments with their parents and makes it more likely they will use these strategies with their peers.

Parents can also help their children to use "positive self-talk". This strategy involves repeating phrases to themselves and coaching themselves to regulate their behavior by saying things such as "keep cool" and "today I'll help others rather than hurt them."

1 About bullying — basics	1	2 Why worry about bullying?	6	3 Bullying: myths, facts and solutions	10
4 Bullying in preschool	14	5 Elementary school children and bullying	19	6 Adolescents and bullying	25
7 Electronic bullying	30	8 Children who bully — what to do at home	36	9 What parents can do to help children who are victimized	40
10 How parents can work with the school	44	11 Bullying prevention through The Golden Rule	48	12 Resources for parents	52

Build positive leadership skills

Power is the ability to influence others' thoughts and behavior. Because bullying has been associated with seeking power, teaching children how to use power in positive ways is essential. Foster positive leadership skills by having your child teach a sibling or younger child a new sport or skill. Teach your child that real leaders treat the people around them with respect.

Reinforcing the positive – Children and teens need to have their strengths recognized and need to be praised for their positive behavior in order to increase the chances of their behaving positively more often. Encourage positive relationships among children by praising cooperative behavior whenever you see it.

Another way to foster strengths is to encourage your child to enroll in organized sports, lessons, camps, and other activities outside of school so they can experience different friendships in different settings. Your child might benefit from being involved in the community by volunteering, which teaches children that they are important and can make a positive contribution. This helps teach your child to care about the rights and needs of others, which in turn helps to cultivate empathy skills.

Developing critical thinking about the media

There are many television shows, movies and video games that promote or glorify violence and aggression as a way of getting what you want. As a parent, it is important to notice and be involved in what your children are exposed to in order to talk about the messages that are delivered. Help your child develop a critical opinion about what messages the media are sending.

1	About bullying — basics	1	2	Why worry about bullying?	6	3	Bullying: myths, facts and solutions	10
4	Bullying in preschool	14	5	Elementary school children and bullying	19	6	Adolescents and bullying	25
7	Electronic bullying	30	8	Children who bully — what to do at home	36	9	What parents can do to help children who are victimized	40
10	How parents can work with the school	44	11	Bullying prevention through The Golden Rule	48	12	Resources for parents	52

Sometimes it is challenging to deal with our children when they are bullying others. Remember that you are an important role model, support, and coach who can significantly influence how your child behaves in relationships. If you use physical discipline at home, ask yourself if the type and degree of discipline that you are using is in fact effective in developing desirable behavior patterns in your child, who may be learning to copy you, or should you take a different approach to discipline at home? Addressing bullying is challenging, but essential. Learning how to treat others respectfully is a process. Your job as a parent is to keep working at teaching this. However long it takes, the results, when you start to see them, are worth the effort.

Used with permission of the creator, Justin Harris.

1 About bullying — basics	1	2 Why worry about bullying?	6	3 Bullying: myths, facts and solutions	10
4 Bullying in preschool	14	5 Elementary school children and bullying	19	6 Adolescents and bullying	25
7 Electronic bullying	30	8 Children who bully — what to do at home	36	9 What parents can do to help children who are victimized	40
10 How parents can work with the school	44	11 Bullying prevention through The Golden Rule	48	12 Resources for parents	52

CHAPTER 9
What parents can do to help children who are victimized

When a child is being bullied, parents often feel that they don't know what they can do to help, or even whether they should intervene at all. In fact, **parents can make a difference and should always intervene.** Since bullying represents a power imbalance, children need parents to support them, to right the power imbalance by providing support to the child, and taking action on the child's behalf. There are many ways a parent can help. Parents should listen to the child and not deny or minimize the child's experience of being bullied. To help the child cope with the experience of being bullied, the parent should also speak up for the child at the school or organization where the bullying takes place. Acting as a role model and helping the child build friendships are also helpful steps to take.

Parents can make a difference by: building strong relationships, teaching coping skills, making the friendship connection and reflecting on parenting styles, as we describe in the following sections.

Building strong relationships

A parent's relationship with his/her child is an important factor in the child's sense of self. When you have a relationship with your child that is built on a foundation of mutual trust and respect, it increases the chances that he or she will tell you about problems at school. If you know there is a problem, then you can work together to address it.

- Make sure your children know how great you think they are! Consistently praise the respectful and cooperative behaviors that you want to see.

1	About bullying — basics	1	2	Why worry about bullying?	6	3	Bullying: myths, facts and solutions	10
4	Bullying in preschool	14	5	Elementary school children and bullying	19	6	Adolescents and bullying	25
7	Electronic bullying	30	8	Children who bully — what to do at home	36	9	What parents can do to help children who are victimized	40
10	How parents can work with the school	44	11	Bullying prevention through The Golden Rule	48	12	Resources for parents	52

- Tell your children you love them as often as you can.

- Connect and communicate with your children. Let them know they can talk to you about anything. Show your children your respect by carefully listening to their concerns.

- Remember that when a child is in trouble or misbehaves, he or she needs you the most. Try to gain an understanding of what the root of the misbehaviour is.

- Wait to be asked. Allow children to ask for help and advice when they need it, rather than offering it when you feel they need it.

- Ask your child about the kind of support that would be helpful and do your best to provide it.

Work with your child to solve problems rather than solving problems for him or her.

A child with you on his or her team is better equipped to handle relationship problems with peers.

Teaching coping skills

Bullying is a relationship problem that can only be solved by making changes to relationships. To deal with bullying, children need to learn and practice skills that will help them develop more positive relationships with peers.

- Give your child phrases he or she can use in bullying situations, as well as words to describe feelings. Demonstrate what you might do or say in response to a bullying episode, and have your child practice using his or her own words.

1 About bullying — basics	1	2 Why worry about bullying?	6	3 Bullying: myths, facts and solutions	10
4 Bullying in preschool	14	5 Elementary school children and bullying	19	6 Adolescents and bullying	25
7 Electronic bullying	30	8 Children who bully — what to do at home	36	9 What parents can do to help children who are victimized	40
10 How parents can work with the school	44	11 Bullying prevention through The Golden Rule	48	12 Resources for parents	52

- With your child, practice different strategies that can be used if he/she is bullied or sees another child being bullied. If your child is being bullied he/she could say: "This is bullying. Stop it now and leave me alone." If your child sees bullying happen, he/she can be part of the solution by showing that the child who is being bullied is not alone. Another important goal when your child wants to help is to get the bullied child away from the bullying situation. Your child could approach the child who is being bullied and say, "Come on, let's go somewhere so that we can play/talk/have lunch together" or, "I'm so glad to see you. I wanted to talk with you. Let's go somewhere else."
- Demonstrate what you might do or say in response to a bullying episode, and have your child practice these same behaviors, using his or her own assertive, not aggressive, words for responding to the bully's actions.
- Teach your children about respectful relationships by talking about behaviors that are acceptable and unacceptable.
- Teach your child how to ask for help.
- Identify someone your child can ask for help at school.
- Talk about what your child can do to comfort another child who has been hurt.

Making the friendship connection

Positive friendships are important for children to grow up happy and strong.

- Create opportunities for your child to practice using relationship skills in different settings, either in sports, lessons or other activi-

1	About bullying — basics	1	2	Why worry about bullying?	6	3	Bullying: myths, facts and solutions	10
4	Bullying in preschool	14	5	Elementary school children and bullying	19	6	Adolescents and bullying	25
7	Electronic bullying	30	8	Children who bully — what to do at home	36	9	What parents can do to help children who are victimized	40
10	How parents can work with the school	44	11	Bullying prevention through The Golden Rule	48	12	Resources for parents	52

ties. Participation in organized activities in and out of school provides children with different places to practice and succeed socially.

- When choosing activities, build on your child's strengths. Choose activities that allow your child to explore new skills and discover his or her talents in order to build self-esteem.
- Keep track of what your child is doing and who he/she is with.

Reflecting on parenting styles

Reflecting on what you may be teaching your kids -- without even realizing it -- can be helpful. This can be hard because it means reflecting on your own thoughts, words, facial expressions, tone of voice, body language and behaviors. It is important to think about the messages these things convey intentionally or unintentionally.

- Provide a model of positive problem solving. Every day children learn by watching their parents. Set a good example by coping with frustration, solving problems and resolving conflicts in positive, productive ways.
- Consider your own behavior in relationships with others. Does the model that you provide show respectful and empathic actions, or critical and aggressive behaviors? Try to provide a model of the relationship skills you want your children to use.
- Admit your mistakes and apologize when your behavior sets a bad example.

Teach your children about their rights in a relationship, what they should expect in their relationships with others and how they deserve to be treated. This will help them to walk away from hurtful relationships.

1	About bullying — basics	**1**	2	Why worry about bullying?	**6**	3	Bullying: myths, facts and solutions	**10**
4	Bullying in preschool	**14**	5	Elementary school children and bullying	**19**	6	Adolescents and bullying	**25**
7	Electronic bullying	**30**	8	Children who bully — what to do at home	**36**	9	What parents can do to help children who are victimized	**40**
10	How parents can work with the school	**44**	11	Bullying prevention through The Golden Rule	**48**	12	Resources for parents	**52**

CHAPTER 10
How parents can work with the school

Parents and caregivers play an important role in responding to bullying behavior. Parents are role models and coaches for their children, as well as advocates speaking up on behalf of their children. When addressing bullying problems, parents need to work collaboratively with the school to ensure that the bullying has stopped.

How and when to approach your school?

Parents need to take bullying concerns seriously and approach the school in a calm, supportive manner. This can be difficult if you are feeling anxious or upset by the bullying, but **it is important to avoid blaming the child who was bullying or the school.** Stay focused on solving the problem. It is critical that you get details of the bullying behaviors: date, time, location, people involved, how it occurred and evidence, if there is any.

Approach the school once you have noticed signs of bullying and have talked with your child. Your goal is to ensure your child's safety and discuss ways to end the bullying. Prior to making contact with the school, reassure your child that it is not his/her fault, and that he/she can walk away and talk to you or another adult about the bullying. Children may be fearful or anxious of parent–school interventions. Discuss approaching the school with your child so that he/she understands that adults can help solve a problem only if they know about it. Depending on the age of your child, you may want to brainstorm which adults you can talk to and work collaboratively to select a person at school that your child trusts.

1	About bullying — basics	1	2	Why worry about bullying?	6	3	Bullying: myths, facts and solutions	10
4	Bullying in preschool	14	5	Elementary school children and bullying	19	6	Adolescents and bullying	25
7	Electronic bullying	30	8	Children who bully — what to do at home	36	9	What parents can do to help children who are victimized	40
10	How parents can work with the school	44	11	Bullying prevention through The Golden Rule	48	12	Resources for parents	52

Talking with the teacher

If you talk with a teacher, plan ahead to identify concerns and suggestions you can bring. Consider what you would like as an outcome of the meeting. Teachers and school staff are in a powerful position to promote healthy relationships and to intervene in bullying situations.

Steps to take:

1. Identify the details of the bullying, as well as any patterns you notice.
2. Work with your child and the teacher to identify solutions, such as someone who can be an ally for your child.
3. Consult widely and think broadly and creatively about ways your child's confidence can be developed.
4. Lastly, identify ways by which you can continue to monitor the situation.

Find out what types of bullying prevention programs and strategies the teacher has participated in. Teachers who have participated in bullying prevention programs feel more confident about handling bullying problems, have more supportive attitudes about victimized students, and feel more positively about working with parents regarding bullying.

Questions to consider:

- Has the teacher discussed bullying with the class?
- Are there class rules about student behaviour?

1 About bullying — basics	1	2 Why worry about bullying?	6	3 Bullying: myths, facts and solutions	10
4 Bullying in preschool	14	5 Elementary school children and bullying	19	6 Adolescents and bullying	25
7 Electronic bullying	30	8 Children who bully — what to do at home	36	9 What parents can do to help children who are victimized	40
10 How parents can work with the school	44	11 Bullying prevention through The Golden Rule	48	12 Resources for parents	52

- What strategies are in place to foster respect or caring for others?
- Is the teacher aware of the bullying prevention policies at their school and the school code of conduct?
- Is there a school-based bullying prevention program in place?
- Does the teacher use cooperative learning tasks and are positive social behaviours being reinforced?

Talking with an administrator

Talking with an administrator is another route. The principal's commitment to allocate time and resources to bullying- prevention-related activities is a key part of ensuring a safe environment for all students. The administrator should be able to discuss with you the school's bullying-prevention policy and can be a good source to find out what services are available to you, your child, the class and the school.

Ask to see the school code of conduct (this code states how people should behave towards one another) and identify specific ways that the child who was bullying may be in violation of this code. Consider asking how the administrator uses progressive discipline to promote a positive school climate. Lastly, find out if there are any bullying-prevention initiatives in which you can participate.

Making a safety plan

A safety plan provides emotional, psychological and practical support for the child who has been victimized while also building awareness and designating a coordinated response in the event of a bullying incident. Making a safety plan is a first step in teaching

1 About bullying — basics	1	2 Why worry about bullying?	6	3 Bullying: myths, facts and solutions	10
4 Bullying in preschool	14	5 Elementary school children and bullying	19	6 Adolescents and bullying	25
7 Electronic bullying	30	8 Children who bully — what to do at home	36	9 What parents can do to help children who are victimized	40
10 How parents can work with the school	44	11 Bullying prevention through The Golden Rule	48	12 Resources for parents	52

self-protection and reminds your child that he/she is not alone. A Safety Plan might include:

- possible routes your child can take to avoid the place where bullying has occurred
- designated increased adult supervision
- and a documented communication plan between home and school.

The Safety Plan can also state steps the teacher/administrator has agreed to take and when police will be contacted, if your child's safety is threatened.

Following up with the school

Effective communication and resolution requires attentive follow up. Parents can work with the school by establishing a communication plan. This plan should include written communication exchanges through emails or notes, pre-arranged meetings face-to-face or on the phone, and a schedule for exchanging messages by email or phone as well as one for meeting face-to-face. It is important that parents find a strategy that works well for them, and for the school personnel involved. Following up with the school helps to communicate a consistent message that bullying is not acceptable, is treated seriously, and it ensures that it will stop. If, when following up, you are not satisfied with the school's response, you may contact the supervisory officer at the local school board.

1	About bullying — basics	1	2	Why worry about bullying?	6	3	Bullying: myths, facts and solutions	10
4	Bullying in preschool	14	5	Elementary school children and bullying	19	6	Adolescents and bullying	25
7	Electronic bullying	30	8	Children who bully — what to do at home	36	9	What parents can do to help children who are victimized	40
10	How parents can work with the school	44	11	Bullying prevention through The Golden Rule	48	12	Resources for parents	52

CHAPTER 11
Bullying prevention through The Golden Rule

Stopping bullying before it becomes a problem

Parents and caregivers socialize children. They teach and help them develop the skills they need to adapt to life outside the family. Some of these lessons take the form of direct teaching and explaining, and some take the form of actions. Adults are role models for children who learn by watching and imitating. If adults engage in healthy relationships and treat others respectfully, so will children.

Children learn by trial and error, and they need many learning opportunities and the patience and support of caring adults to develop healthy relationship skills. Very few of us learn things the first time we try them and learning how to have healthy relationships is complex. But, having healthy relationships is one of the best ways to prevent bullying from happening in the first place.

Preventing bullying by practicing the Golden Rule

From preschool onwards, children can begin to think about and talk about emotions, such as happiness, sadness, and fear, and they can come to understand that these emotions are experienced by everyone. This is the foundation for the Golden Rule, which is the basis upon which all healthy relationships rest.

THE GOLDEN RULE: Treat others the same way you want them to treat you.

1	About bullying — basics	1	2	Why worry about bullying?	6	3	Bullying: myths, facts and solutions	10
4	Bullying in preschool	14	5	Elementary school children and bullying	19	6	Adolescents and bullying	25
7	Electronic bullying	30	8	Children who bully — what to do at home	36	9	What parents can do to help children who are victimized	40
10	How parents can work with the school	44	11	Bullying prevention through The Golden Rule	48	12	Resources for parents	52

- **Teach children of all ages the Golden Rule:** *"Treat others the same way you want them to treat you."* Say it often. Expand upon the message, saying, *"You are important and your feelings are important. You want to be happy, and to be treated with respect and kindness. Everyone wants to be happy and treated with respect and kindness. You know what makes you happy and makes you sad. So you know what will make others feel happy and sad."*

- **Be a role model** and try hard to show respect and kindness in all your interactions. Use the Golden Rule to reflect upon your own behavior. Ask yourself, *"Am I treating others the way I want the children in my care to treat each other?"*

- **Watch children as they interact with one another and act on "teachable moments".** Describe the behavior you want to see and help children understand what you mean by respect (listening when others speak, taking turns, sharing, acting fairly, following the rules, etc.) and kindness (saying nice things, helping, including, encouraging, welcoming, etc.).

- **Give clear praise that focuses on a behavior.** Whenever you see respectful or kind behavior, praise it while saying exactly what it is that you are praising. Effective praise means clearly describing the specific behavior and praising it. For example, *"You listened to Daniel and shared your toys. What a fantastic way to show respect!"* Or, *"You helped Sophie climb up the stairs. That was so kind of you!"* Praise is a powerful, positive reinforcement. The more often you use positive reinforcement, the more often your child will use respectful and kind behaviors in the future.

- Use the Golden Rule to help children understand that disrespectful and unkind behavior hurts and we don't want people to hurt us. Explain that some things hurt our bodies (pushing or hitting) and

1	About bullying — basics	**1**	2	Why worry about bullying?	**6**	3	Bullying: myths, facts and solutions	**10**
4	Bullying in preschool	**14**	5	Elementary school children and bullying	**19**	6	Adolescents and bullying	**25**
7	Electronic bullying	**30**	8	Children who bully — what to do at home	**36**	9	What parents can do to help children who are victimized	**40**
10	How parents can work with the school	**44**	11	Bullying prevention through The Golden Rule	**48**	12	Resources for parents	**52**

some things hurt our feelings (saying bad things or not including someone). Because these things hurt when they happen to us, we know that these things hurt when they happen to other people too. Because we know how it feels, we know that we should not do hurtful things to others.

- Explain to all children and teens, in age-appropriate language, that it is their right to feel respected and safe when they are with others. Help them develop an expectation that adults will help them. Tell them *"If someone hurts your body or your feelings, you should tell him/her to follow the Golden Rule Rule that you should treat other people the way you want to be treated. If they don't stop and you feel sad or scared, then you should tell me (or your teacher). I (or your teacher) will help you solve the problem and feel better."* Growing up with an expectation of respect and safety will help your child/teenager develop an understanding of the concept of human rights.

- **Use the Golden Rule to correct and coach.** Recognize and label hurtful behavior when you see it. Labeling a bullying child's hurtful words as "hurtful" or "unkind" supports the victimized child by helping him/her put a name to and thus understand what he/she has experienced. This helps the victimized child cope with the experience. It also provides a learning opportunity and sends a message to the children watching the bullying. They learn that hurting others is unacceptable behavior. The next step is that they can be encouraged to think about how to make things right for the victimized child.

- **The Golden Rule is equally important for peers who may not be directly involved in bullying, but see it happening.** Peers who watch bullying are inadvertently supporting the child who is

1	About bullying — basics	1	2	Why worry about bullying?	6	3	Bullying: myths, facts and solutions	10
4	Bullying in preschool	14	5	Elementary school children and bullying	19	6	Adolescents and bullying	25
7	Electronic bullying	30	8	Children who bully — what to do at home	36	9	What parents can do to help children who are victimized	40
10	How parents can work with the school	44	11	Bullying prevention through The Golden Rule	48	12	Resources for parents	52

bullying by giving him/her attention. Instead, bystanders need to live by the Golden Rule and stand up for the child being victimized. This is challenging, but peers who stand up for others are an important part of the solution. If they stand by and do nothing and watch, they are part of the problem.

- Living by the Golden Rule means that you treat other people the way you want to be treated

Used with permission.

1	About bullying — basics	1	2	Why worry about bullying?	6	3	Bullying: myths, facts and solutions	10
4	Bullying in preschool	14	5	Elementary school children and bullying	19	6	Adolescents and bullying	25
7	Electronic bullying	30	8	Children who bully — what to do at home	36	9	What parents can do to help children who are victimized	40
10	How parents can work with the school	44	11	Bullying prevention through The Golden Rule	48	12	Resources for parents	52

CHAPTER 12
Resources for parents

Books

- Agaston, P., Kowalski, R. & Limber, S. Cyberbullying: Bullying in the Digital Age .Wiley-Blackwell Press, 2007.

- Alexander, J. When Your Child is Bullied. Pocket Books, 2006.

- Baris, M., Garrity, C., & Porter, W. Bully Proofing Your Child: A Parent's Guide, 2000.

- Bott, C. J. The Bully in the Book and in the Classroom. Scarecrow Press, 2004.

- Coloroso, B. The Bully, The Bullied, and The Bystander: From Preschool to High School– How Parents & Teachers Can Help Break the Cycle of Violence. Harper Collins, 2002.

- Coloroso, B. The Bully, the Bullied, and the Bystander. Harper Collins, 2004.

- De Lara, E., Garbarino, J. And Words Can Hurt Forever: How to Protect Adolescents from Bullying. Free Press, 2002.

- Freedman, J.S. Easing the Teasing: Helping Your Child Cope with Name-Calling, Ridicule, and Verbal Bullying. McGraw-Hill, 2002.

- Goleman, D. Social Intelligence: The New Science of Human Relationships. Bantam, 2006

- Horne, A.,Whitford, J.L. & Bell, C.D. Parents Guide to Understanding & Responding to Bullying: The Bully Buster's Approach. Research Press, 2007

1 About bullying — basics	1	2 Why worry about bullying?	6	3 Bullying: myths, facts and solutions	10
4 Bullying in preschool	14	5 Elementary school children and bullying	19	6 Adolescents and bullying	25
7 Electronic bullying	30	8 Children who bully — what to do at home	36	9 What parents can do to help children who are victimized	40
10 How parents can work with the school	44	11 Bullying prevention through The Golden Rule	48	12 Resources for parents	52

- Lajoie, G., McLellan, A., Seddon, C. How Parents Can Take Action Against Bullying. Bully B'ware Productions, 2000.

- Olweus, D. Bullying at School: What We Know and What We Can Do. Blackwell Publishers, 1993.

- Rigby, K. Children and Bullying: How Parents and Educators Can Reduce the Risk of Bullying in Schools. Blackwell/Wiley, 2008.

- Roberts, A. Safe Teen: Powerful Alternatives to Violence. Polestar Book Publishers, 2001.

- Sullivan, K. The Anti-Bullying Handbook. Oxford University Press, 2000.

- Tippins, S., Sheras, P. Your Child: Bully or Victim? Understanding and Ending Schoolyard Tyranny. Skylight Press, 2002.

- Voors, W. The Parent's Book About Bullying: Changing the Course of Your Child's Life. Hazelden, 2000.

- Willard, N.E. Cyberbullying and Cyberthreats. Research Press, 2007.

Videos:

- Cyber-bullying   http://youtube/Hdvhe0Nqqek

- Signs Your Child is Being Bullied   http://youtube/nUiqUlHNHa0

- Public Service Announcements from Concerned Children's Advertisers   http://www.cca-kids.ca/english/psas/bullying_prevention.html

- The Myths of Bullying   http://youtube/H5kPeGFt34Y

#	Topic	Page	#	Topic	Page	#	Topic	Page
1	About bullying — basics	1	2	Why worry about bullying?	6	3	Bullying: myths, facts and solutions	10
4	Bullying in preschool	14	5	Elementary school children and bullying	19	6	Adolescents and bullying	25
7	Electronic bullying	30	8	Children who bully — what to do at home	36	9	What parents can do to help children who are victimized	40
10	How parents can work with the school	44	11	Bullying prevention through The Golden Rule	48	12	Resources for parents	52

- What to Do if Your Child Bullies?
  http://www.youtube.com/watch?v=xgFN-mU9wVU&feature=relmfu
- What Parents Need to Do In Schools
  http://www.youtube.com/watch?v=URsjAvx6zzo&list=PLB487334673EDE3C4&index=9&feature=plpp_video
- Why Do Children Bully Others?
  http://www.youtube.com/watch?feature=player_embedded&v=ZSQRfsvKUHE#

Websites:
Here are examples of North American websites with a strong research foundation that have created resources specifically for parents.

- About Kids Health is a resource for all issues on children's health, including bullying   http://www.aboutkidshealth.ca/En/HealthAZ/FamilyandPeerRelations/PeerRelations/Pages/Bullying.aspx
- Concerned Children's Advertisers: Giving Canadian children tools to be media and life wise   http://play.longlivekids.ca/parent
- Cyberbullying Research Center   http://cyberbullying.us/
- MediaSmarts: Canada's Centre for Digital and Media Literacy   http://mediasmarts.ca/
- Net Cetera: Chatting with Kids About Being Online
  http://www.ftc.gov/bcp/edu/pubs/consumer/tech/tec04.pdf
- PACER is an organization for parents and youth who have disabilities, with guidelines for dealing with bullying problems.
  http://www.pacer.org/bullying/

1 About bullying — basics	1	2 Why worry about bullying?	6	3 Bullying: myths, facts and solutions	10
4 Bullying in preschool	14	5 Elementary school children and bullying	19	6 Adolescents and bullying	25
7 Electronic bullying	30	8 Children who bully — what to do at home	36	9 What parents can do to help children who are victimized	40
10 How parents can work with the school	44	11 Bullying prevention through The Golden Rule	48	12 Resources for parents	52

- Promoting Relationships and Eliminating Violence Network (PREVNet): Canada's authority on research and resources for bullying prevention: www.prevnet.ca

- teachsafeschools: A website whose mission is to help school personnel develop a supportive, safe and inviting learning environment www.teachsafeschools.org

- United States Department of Health and Human Services – Stop Bullying Now   http://www.stopbullying.gov/

- In addition to national and federal government organizations in the United States and Canada that are focused on bullying prevention, there are similar programs and resources at the state/province/city/local area level. To find ones close to you, google "bullying prevention" and include your state/province/city/town/local area.

Used with permission.

1	About bullying — basics	1	2	Why worry about bullying?	6	3	Bullying: myths, facts and solutions	10
4	Bullying in preschool	14	5	Elementary school children and bullying	19	6	Adolescents and bullying	25
7	Electronic bullying	30	8	Children who bully — what to do at home	36	9	What parents can do to help children who are victimized	40
10	How parents can work with the school	44	11	Bullying prevention through The Golden Rule	48	12	Resources for parents	52

CPSIA information can be obtained
at www.ICGtesting.com
Printed in the USA
LVIW02n1417181013
357590LV00027B/192